AUSTRALIAN WOODCUTS
AND LINOCUTS
of the 1920s and 1930s

Nicholas Draffin

SUN·ACADEMY SERIES

Front cover:
Waratahs (c. 1930)
Hand-coloured woodcut by Margaret Preston

Title page:
Satan
Wood engraving by Lionel Lindsay

Back cover:
The Jester (1923)
(Self-portrait in Fancy Dress)
Wood engraving by Lionel Lindsay

Sun Books Pty Ltd
South Melbourne, Victoria 3205, Australia
First published by Sun Books 1976
Copyright © text Nicholas Draffin

National Library of Australia
cataloguing in publication data

Draffin, Nicholas
    Australian woodcuts and linocuts of the 1920s and
    1930s

    ISBN 0 7251 0224 1.

    1. Wood-engravings, Australian.
    2. Linoleum block-printing.
    I. Title.

769.994

Set in Times
by Monotrade, Melbourne
Printed in Hong Kong

Lionel Lindsay's wood engraving tools

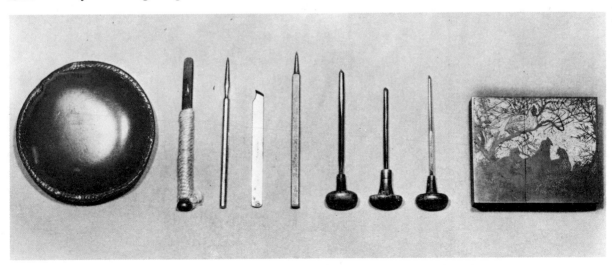

oodblocking, said Margaret Preston in 1930, 'is a comfortable kind of craft . . . one of the easiest of all the crafts in the way of materials. Anyone can have them.' One might add that woodcut is not only one of the simplest ways of making prints but also the oldest. In Europe, particularly in Germany, the craft was developed in the fifteenth century; the Chinese used the technique some centuries earlier. The convenience with which a woodblock can be set with a body of movable type and printed in a single operation led to widespread use of woodcuts for illustrating books and broadsheets. A number of noted artists, Albrecht Dürer outstanding amongst them, responded to the capacity of the medium to express their own graphic genius. Later, in the seventeenth and eighteenth centuries, woodcut was superseded in popularity by the process of line engraving. Artists employed the techniques of etching and engraving, particularly etching with its direct and vivid qualities, its capacity for fine line and tonal effects.

In the nineteenth century there was a strong revival of the craft of woodcutting and a widespread use of wood engravings to illustrate the ever-increasing numbers of illustrated books and newspapers. These were being produced for a market that was rapidly expanding as the number of literate people increased at an unprecedented rate. The quality of work ranged from the crude, popular cuts illustrating broadsheets and ballads and the uninspired hack work for the cheapest books and papers to the fine and sensitive work produced by the Dalziel brothers, who in the sixties reproduced designs by Millais, Rossetti, Sandys and other pre-Raphaelites. In most cases, the woodcuts and wood engravings were reproductive, based on designs by other artists, and were used as book or magazine illustrations. The development of the techniques purely for their artistic potential seldom occurred before the end of the century.

Woodcuts probably appeared in Australia shortly after the first printing press began to produce proclamations, newspapers and books. Woodcuts produced in Australia in the nineteenth century are of little artistic interest, and only a few brief notes will be offered here. Their detailed study can be left to bibliographers, historians and Australianaographers. High quality illustration was to be the province of the lithographic printer, and the most important artists were to use lithography as their chosen medium of printmaking. Conrad Martens published several albums of lithographs, while Eugene von Guerard, Nicholas Chevalier and S. T. Gill worked in collaboration with lithographic printers to produce albums of chromolithographs that remain among the most important examples of nineteenth century Australian printmaking. By comparison, woodcut and wood engraving produced few memorable individuals. One might single out Samuel Calvert, whose father Edward Calvert had been one of the Ancients—the group of young English artists inspired by their contact with William Blake. Unlike his father, who in his lifetime in England produced a small but quite remarkable body of work, Samuel seems to have been engaged actively in Australia in reproductive work and illustration for Melbourne newspapers. He is best remembered for a large panoramic view of Melbourne (1871) and wood engravings reproducing paintings by Buvelot. The brothers Arthur and George Collingridge, who arrived in Australia in the late 1870s, seem to have dominated the craft of wood engraving in Sydney. Although Arthur died in 1907, George lived to the age of eighty-two and exhibited works in the 1920s, when he was admired and received suitable respect as one of the 'elders' of the tribe of woodcut artists. There is no space to mention other individuals working at this period, but it is worth noting that *The Picturesque Atlas of Australasia* published in Sydney in 1886 contains a very large number of wood engravings based on drawings by various artists. The illustrated papers retained wood engravers to produce illustrations, and Hall Thorpe, one of the artists illustrated in this book, began his career in 1891 with a four year apprenticeship in drawing and engraving on wood with John Fairfax and Sons. The 1890s were to see the end of the use of woodcut and wood engraving for illustrations in newspapers following the invention of photo-mechanical means to reproduce drawings and later photographs. The obsolescence of the techniques may have left able craftsmen without work but combined with influences from overseas it left the field free for new experiment with the artistic possibilities of woodcut and wood engraving. After a pause of some years there was a sudden efflorescence of woodcuts and wood engravings that began in the early 1920s and continued with some vigour for nearly two decades.

The examples of woodcut and wood engraving known to Australian artists at the beginning of this century as a form of artistic expression were predominantly English, although it is worth mentioning that by the late 1860s the Melbourne Public Library owned a copy of Albrecht Dürer's woodcuts and had published a lithographic facsimile of this work. It was the work of the Englishman Thomas Bewick (1753–1827) that gave Lionel Lindsay his first inspiration for wood engraving, and Bewick and William Blake were the subject of the first articles on wood engraving to appear in *Art in Australia*. Bewick, Blake and Edward Calvert were the three significant artists who did original wood engravings at the beginning of the nineteenth century. The Dalziel brothers, who in the 1860s were working from designs by the pre-Raphaelites, inspired Ernest Moffit and Norman and Lionel Lindsay to their first essays in woodcut but seem to have had little subsequent effect. Napier Waller was influenced by the works of the pre-Raphaelites and may possibly have known the woodcuts produced in England for the Kelmscott Press publications by William Morris and Edward Burne-Jones. The example of the Kelmscott Press produced a sudden outburst of beautiful books with woodcut illustrations, including the work of Charles Ricketts and Charles Shannon. The revival of woodcut in England remained tied to fine book production until at least the beginning of this century.

From 1893 new developments in English art were publicized in a new magazine called *The Studio*, and it appears that as each new copy of *The Studio* arrived in Australia it was eagerly examined by progressive artists and art students. Of particular interest to the present study is a special volume published in 1919, *Modern Woodcuts and Lithographs (by French and British Artists)*. Two Australian-born artists were included in the illustrations— Hall Thorpe, who had settled in London and was establishing a workshop that produced modern decorative woodcuts, and Thea Proctor, who had made a reputation in London as a lithographer. Of greater importance were the examples of modern woodcuts that were illustrated. It seems that this volume acted as a source book for the sudden outburst of woodcuts in Australia in the early 1920s. A 1927 Studio publication, *The Woodcut of Today at Home and Abroad* may have maintained the strength of the movement, but by that date woodcuts had been well established in Australia and the influence was accordingly less.

Australian artists seem to have been chiefly influenced by English and, to a lesser extent, French examples. Japanese woodcuts were known and admired in Australia in the twenties and thirties but seem to have had less direct influence on local artists. The influence was largely mediated through English and French woodcut artists experimenting with the Japanese style. The prolific activity in Germany, particularly the radically innovative works of the expressionist artists, seems to have been little known, partly due to Australia's geographical isolation but perhaps also because of the strong anti-German prejudices generated in the First World War. The only artist represented in this book who shows the direct influence of German expressionism is Ludwig Hirschfeld Mack. He arrived in Australia in 1940 and spent his first years here in internment camps for German aliens. The Australian artists who studied abroad generally worked in London and in a few instances in Paris.

efore looking at the sudden development of woodcut in Australia, a few words may be said about the techniques used to make prints. They are fairly simple and may already be familiar to readers. In all cases the design is printed from the surface of the block. Areas that are not to be printed are cut away by various means, and the design is left standing as a flat surface in relief. Once the block has been cut the surface is inked, a piece of paper is laid upon it and the ink is transferred from the block to the paper under pressure.

An artist using the woodcut technique uses a smooth, flat piece of wood that is usually cut along the grain like a plank and planed smooth. The design is generally drawn on the wood and sharp knives are used to cut around the edge of the design. Areas that are to appear white on the final print may then be cut away with a knife or gouged out with gougers and chisels. A relatively soft, close-textured wood is normally used, since more coarsely textured timbers tend to show the grain of the wood on the print. However, the wood grain was later incorporated in the design to add character to the print. In early German and in Japanese woodcuts the design was often drawn by the artist and the cutting done by specially trained craftsmen, perhaps under the close supervision of the artist. In the period considered by this book the artists almost invariably cut their own blocks as well as supervising the printing. It is possible to cut directly on to the block without first drawing a preliminary design. Margaret Preston was one artist who used this technique, allowing the character of the woodblock to determine to some extent the final appearance of the print. In a number of cases artists have used wood that is cut across the grain rather than along the grain. Margaret Preston's block for *Wheel Flower* is made up of nine such end-grain blocks fastened together but cut as for a standard woodcut.

Wood engraving, as opposed to woodcut, invariably uses end-grain blocks. They are generally of a hard, close-textured wood, the most preferred kind being Turkish boxwood. The block is then worked with engraver's tools—the burin, the scorper, the tint-tool— to give a fine design of white lines against the black of the surface of the block. Lionel Lindsay, following the examples of Bewick, William Blake and the brothers Dalziel, used this technique almost exclusively in his published work. Fine examples of the technique can also be seen in Helen Ogilvie's work. Again, large areas that are to appear white in the final print are cut away with gougers and chisels. The size of the print is dictated by the size of the block available—boxwood blocks are not usually very large, but in some cases a number of blocks are carefully fitted together to form one larger block.

There is, then, a simple distinction between woodcuts and wood engravings. In woodcuts the areas of black and white are differentiated by cutting with a knife and gouging with a chisel. In wood engravings white lines are produced by making incisions into the areas of the block that would otherwise print black. In practice, the distinction is blurred by the technical inventiveness of artists. While it may be difficult to use engraving tools on blocks cut along the plank for woodcut, the cutter may use his knife and chisels with great delicacy to approximate the fine lines most characteristic of engraving, and the wood engraver may make free use of knives and gougers on an end-grain block as well as using engraving techniques. While wood is the material most commonly employed, the artist may use other materials—metal blocks, celluloid, or anything else that is convenient—but still use the techniques of woodcut and wood engraving. Among Eric Thake's first works are prints made from blocks of stereotype metal cut as for a woodcut or wood engraving.

Linocuts are made in much the same way as woodcuts. The design is cut out with a sharp knife, and the areas to appear white on the print are then cut away with gouges. The technique is a relatively modern one. Linoleum was only invented in the mid-nineteenth century and apparently only used for making prints after the beginning of this century, perhaps after the First World War. The term 'linocut' seems to have come into use at the beginning of the 1920s. Linocuts may sometimes be considered the poor man's woodcut. By 1920 a suitable grade of linoleum adapted to printing became available, and it was close-textured, softer and more easily worked than wooden blocks. By 1930 it was coming into its own, particularly as used by Claude Flight and his followers in England. Probably the most outstanding examples of colour linocut were made by Picasso in the early 1950s. Now, in the mid-1970s, linoleum has been superseded by vinyl and other synthetic floor coverings, and linoleum suitable for printing purposes is increasingly hard to obtain. In the period under consideration the craft of linocut was taught extensively in schools. A photograph by Harold Cazneaux shows linocuts being made by pupils at Frensham in the 1930s.

Colour prints could be made by any of the above techniques, although generally wood engraving depended on its use of black and white contrasts for a simple graphic statement. Colour woodcuts, as opposed to hand-coloured woodcuts, were made by using a number of blocks, one for each separate colour. The artists who consciously followed Japanese techniques painstakingly made a series of blocks and printed each separately, using a different colour for each block and inking each carefully. Margaret Preston's first colour prints were made by overprinting a number of specially cut blocks for colour over the key (black) block, although she seems to have soon decided that it was easier to colour each print by hand, perhaps through a stencil. The choice between making a colour print and a hand-coloured print seems to have been a matter of convenience or of personal preference for the artists concerned. Linocut seems to have been most commonly used for colour prints. This may in part be because the linoleum blocks were easier to cut than wood. In a few cases a slightly textured linoleum was used to give a mottled texture to the colour as in some of Napier Waller's colour prints. But the choice also owes much to the example and encouragement of a group of progressive English artists, particularly Claude Flight and his colleagues.

Printing wood and lino blocks is again a simple process. An appropriate ink is rolled across the relief surface of the block, paper is laid over the block and carefully pressed or rubbed to transfer the ink from block to paper. A printing press is not necessary. The back of the paper may be rubbed with a baren (a flat pad as used by Japanese woodcut printers), the back of a kitchen spoon or even the palm of the hand. Margaret Preston considered that the use of a press gave mechanical and insensitive results, and she advocated careful hand printing with a baren. The result is delicate and subtle areas of black. Wood engravers such as Lionel Lindsay preferred to use a press, thus producing a rich and even black surface that accentuates the contrasts of black and white in their prints. The choice of inks and papers also effects the final appearance of the print. Oil-based inks may be used, particularly black lithographers ink for wood engravings. Japanese-inspired colour prints most used were water-based inks. Eveline Syme seems to have been particularly insistent on the use of water-based inks; Ethleen Palmer chose inks that sometimes yield a highly textured rough surface. The paper used for printing is again a matter of individual choice, but there seems to have been a marked preference for Japanese papers, notably a very thin, strong tissue and sometimes a thick, soft white fibrous paper. European papers also occur, ranging from fine hand-made papers to ordinary writing paper, vegetable parchment and even blotting paper.

fter the First World War, in the years following 1920, there occurred in Australia a remarkable flowering of the arts of woodcut and wood engraving and this continued undiminished for at least a decade. From 1930 linocuts, particularly colour linocuts, came into equal prominence. This book is intended to present a visual survey of this important and hitherto neglected aspect of Australian art. The activity covers a fairly clearly defined period between 1920 and 1940. The works in these media dwindled and fell from notice after the outbreak of the Second World War, and since then there has been little serious study or documentation of the period. The early works of Moffitt and the Lindsay brothers were and are little known, and so too are the woodcuts of Blamire Young, who is remembered only for his brilliant watercolours, which were among the best ever painted in Australia. His posters are now forgotten. The colour prints of Violet Teague and Geraldine Rede, which adorn their book of 1905, seem to be entirely forgotten.

Lionel Lindsay played a major part in the development of woodcut in Australia, but developments in England before, during and after the war also exerted a strong influence. Margaret Preston and Thea Proctor had both returned to Australia from England by 1920, and Mrs Preston showed colour woodcuts (made in London) in Sydney in that year. The intellectual climate following the war is of great importance; ideas current in London and Paris were also generated in Australia. The war was the first major conflict in which Australia had played an extensive part, and the resultant upheavals lead to radical changes in social attitudes. Reconstruction after the years of crisis and carnage was imperative, and artists developed fresh and positive attitudes to the influence of works of art on public life. Hall Thorpe, an Australian-born artist working in London, produced several pamphlets extolling the virtues of modern woodcuts for the private home. He stressed their cheerful bright decorative qualities as opposed to the gloomy, depressing and reactionary character of nineteenth-century 'high art' known at second hand through inferior reproductions. Thea Proctor's first woodcuts were made as colourful decorations for children's nurseries, and many of Margaret Preston's woodcuts were produced for their decorative qualities and sold at low prices—rarely as much as four guineas for outstanding works. This makes recent high prices charged for her woodcuts a complete travesty of her original intentions.

Lionel Lindsay's impact on the art world owed most to his role as a highly influential critic, writer and talker, although his example as an artist may well have provided inspiration too. Australia published only one art magazine. This was the new and influentially powerful *Art in Australia*. It ignored woodcuts until 1923, when it printed articles by Lindsay on the English artists Thomas Bewick and William Blake. In the same year it printed an article signed by Sydney Ure Smith—written perhaps with the help from Lionel Lindsay—on 'The Revival of Woodcut in Australia'. It would be more accurate, however, to talk not of a revival of woodcut but a new development. In 1922 Lindsay had produced *A Book of Woodcuts*, the first album of its kind in Australia. In 1923 he organized at Tyrrell's in Sydney the first Australian exhibition devoted entirely to woodcuts. This exhibition included work by Lindsay, Napier Waller, Margaret Preston, Roy Davies, Christian Yandell and George Collingridge. A little earlier in the same year, it was surely Lindsay who was responsible for the inclusion of woodcuts by Lindsay himself, Margaret Preston, and Napier Waller in the exhibition of Australian Art shown in London in Burlington House. From the year 1923 woodcuts were included in the exhibitions of the Society of Artists and given serious critical consideration in the magazine *Art in Australia*.

There is a noticeably high proportion of women among the artists working in woodcut and linocut in this period. Various theories of social change might be advanced to explain this it was certainly, in part at least, a direct result of the war, in which an enormous number of able young men were killed or maimed. The war no doubt catalysed other changes, including more liberal attitudes towards women and greater opportunities for them to pursue independent careers, both of which had first begun to appear at the beginning of the century. Women artists were certainly not a new phenomenon, and in the early years of this century increasing numbers of female students had attended the art schools. It is worth noting that etching, at the height of popularity during the twenties, was almost exclusively the domain of men, and only a few women, among them Jessie Traill and Eirene Mort, were able to achieve any degree of success in this medium. Etching in Australia was to remain a relatively conservative craft, only a few fine works and a host of pedestrian landscapes were produced. There was very little innovative work.

Woodcuts on the other hand inspired some powerful, fresh and original work. Margaret Preston and Thea Proctor were widely respected as the foremost modern artists in Sydney. Even Lionel Lindsay, notably antipathetic to modernism, admired Margaret Preston's work. Thea Proctor, who had ventured into woodcut in 1925, began to teach at the Julian Ashton school and in her own studio. Prints by her students appeared in several issues of *Art in Australia*. These were animated and original and showed a strong feeling for pattern and texture—qualities that were stressed by their teacher. Adelaide Perry also taught linocut and woodcut. Otherwise there seems to have been little teaching available in Australia until late in the thirties, and most artists were either self-taught or had studied in England. English prints of the time became available in Australia. They were brought out and shown by John Young at the Macquarie Gallery and by other dealers. They appeared in such magazines as *The Home* and served as a further impetus to the art.

Some themes recur in the prints of this period. There is a recurrent fascination with barnyard poultry—cocks, hens and turkeys. Some property owners could afford to maintain aviaries of beautiful pheasants, peacocks and parrots. Lionel Lindsay had vivid memories of his boyhood discovery of a whole host of magical and brightly coloured birds kept at the back of an old mansion in Creswick, and 'this vision of exotic beauty' inspired his wood engravings featuring curassows, toucans, peacocks and macaws as well as the less exotic roosters and owls. The rendering of the differing textures of feather and quill, beak and claw, the use of the odd, irregular and baroque forms of the birds and, at times, the endowment of birds with anthropomorphic qualities of alertness, stupidity, confidence or depression appealed not only to Lindsay but to numerous other artists. Margaret Preston firmly resisted these temptations, and her few woodcuts of birds show native species depicted unsentimentally in strong and vigorous contrasts of black and white and sometimes enriched with bold colour.

Flowers and plants were another popular theme. A large part of Hall Thorpe's work shows vases of garden flowers, deliberately chosen for their colourful and cheerful decorative qualities. Margaret Preston's fine studies of flowers are among the best known of her woodcuts. Some are masterly and powerful, others consciously decorative; in most she shows a seriousness of purpose in working consistently from native Australian plants. She was described by Lindsay in 1923 as a 'cosmopolitan', but in fact her style is consciously national. She used native flora and fauna, local landscape and, later, Aboriginal subjects with a deliberate intention of evolving a true Australian style. Her perceptive appreciation of Australian Aboriginal art exerted an increasingly strong influence on her own work.

Birds and flowers are ancient conventional themes in Chinese and Japanese art. Many of the woodcuts showing these subjects may have been indirectly derived from these conventions. Some of Lionel Lindsay's wood engravings show birds and flowers combined with an oriental delicacy of composition and texture that is surely a conscious homage to the arts of the east, for Lindsay developed a high respect and admiration for Chinese art. In other Australian woodcuts the influence is less immediately apparent, but at this time there was an increasing interest in the arts of China and Japan, manifested particularly in the popularity of lacquer work, cane and bamboo, and silk embroideries. The influence is mediated also through European examples, not only in prints but in the other decorative arts. Japanese prints were circulated and collected, and they inspired a few direct imitators in Australia. The West Australian A. B. Webb worked in the mid-twenties to achieve a technique for colour woodcuts in the Japanese manner; Paul Haefliger later experimented with the technique in the mid-thirties. A little later, Ethleen Palmer in Sydney achieved some success, although her best known print, *Spindrift*, is a very self-conscious imitation of the Hokusai woodcut of *The Wave*. In general, the direct imitators of Japanese woodcuts, both in Australia and in Europe, seem to have doomed themselves to genteel oblivion for want of the vital spark of imagination necessary to lift their enormous technical competence above the level of banality.

'Modern' subjects relating to machinery, technological development and busy urban life were not very common in prints of this period, although they came into prominence in paintings executed in the years 1927–1928, especially in Margaret Preston's paintings and writings of this time. The building of the Sydney Harbour Bridge attracted the attention of many artists and inspired fine paintings and etchings but apparently no woodcuts. Modern industry provided subject matter for photographers such as Harold Cazneaux but does not seem to have inspired contemporary painters and printmakers. Ailsa Lee Brown's *Moths over the Quay* is an unexpected and compelling glimpse of the aeroplane as a feature of modern life, and Amy Kingston's *Ship's Ventilators* makes use of the mechanical forms of the ironmongery of ship-building; but they are unusual. Few artists in Australia were concerned to confront the aesthetics of modern machinery. Ethel Spowers' linocut *Wet Afternoon*, an umbrella-scape, and its companion print *The Newsboy*, with its sea of newspapers, are strikingly modern in comparison with other Australian prints of the period and are among Miss Spowers' most imaginative and exciting prints. But umbrellas, familiar in Japanese *ukiyo-e* woodcuts, had already provided inspiration for C. R. W. Nevinson in England and for the French impressionists and post-impressionist before him. While Miss Spowers' contemporaries in England produced striking linocuts of tube stations and machinery, her own progressive work was too far ahead of the taste of her Australian audience, and she apparently destroyed many of her best works out of frustration. In her later years she concentrated on works that would appeal to children.

The Depression in the 1930s contributed to the demise of etching in Australia and perhaps also of woodcuts and linocuts. It has been suggested that the economic conditions of a depression would encourage the production of low-cost works of art, particularly prints. But Sid Long, writing at the end of the 1930s, pointed out that etchings that had once been assured of ready sales now sold slowly, if at all. The same probably applied to woodcuts and linocuts, although Helen Ogilvie remembers her own wood engravings selling well in the mid-1930s at five shillings each. Whatever the reason, after the outbreak of the Second World War in 1939, exhibitions of woodcuts and linocuts virtually ceased. Social and artistic changes produced a new group of young progressive artists, led by William Dobell and Russell Drysdale in the early 1940s, who were not involved in printmaking.

There was no absolute break in continuity. Eric Thake is an important artist who has continued to produce linocuts. Every year he has produced one linocut as a Christmas card. This series, which continues to the present time, and his other later linocuts, drawings, watercolours and paintings are beyond the scope of this present book.

Artists and Illustrations

Blamire Young (1862–1935)

William Blamire Young first arrived in Australia as a young teacher and was persuaded by Phil May to devote his attention to art. He returned to England several times, the first was in 1893 when he came into close contact with the Beggarstaff brothers. He is known chiefly for his watercolours, some of which are among the finest painted in Australia.

Blamire Young's work with the Beggarstaff brothers in London would have given him direct experience of William Nicholson's work in woodcut. After his return to Australia he produced a small number of woodcuts —fewer than half a dozen are known—of which the print illustrated and a companion piece are the earliest. A slightly later example appeared in *The Lone Hand* in 1907.

A Print from Johnny Fawkner's Press (1902)
Woodcut. 15.4 cm × 15.4 cm.
Made for the Library Association, Melbourne, and printed on John Pascoe Fawkner's printing press in the Melbourne Public Library.
National Gallery of Victoria

Lionel Lindsay (1874–1961)

Lionel Lindsay, his brother Norman and their friend Ernest Moffitt first experimented with woodcuts in about 1897. They were inspired by the woodcuts of the brothers Dalziel from designs by the pre-Raphaelites. Lionel Lindsay produced a few more woodcuts in subsequent years and in about 1907 began to experiment with colour woodcuts in the Japanese manner of which *Spanish Woman* is an example. These early adventures in the medium are little known and few examples survive.

In 1922 he turned his attention to wood engraving, largely inspired by the work of Thomas Bewick. He had been moved by an illustration of Bewick's engraving tools as well as by his fine and delicate craftsmanship and was able to acquire the engraving tools that had belonged to the artist John Mather. His publication in 1922 of *A Book of Woodcuts* marked the beginning of a period of concentrated activity in the medium, although he continued at the same time to produce watercolours and etchings. He was represented by three woodcuts in the 1923 London exhibition of Australian art. Working almost invariably on boxwood blocks, he used a fine and classic wood engraving technique, sometimes combining this with simple woodcut techniques; he printed the proofs himself on his own press. In all he produced over two hundred wood engravings, most of them in the period 1922–1939. He is particularly remembered for his fine studies of birds. In technical accomplishment he had few, if any, rivals.

Spanish Woman (c. 1907)
Colour woodcut. 28.9 cm × 14.0 cm. Not published.
Ballarat Fine Art Gallery

Satan (1922)
Wood engraving. 5.3 cm × 4.7 cm.
From *A Book of Woodcuts*, Sydney, 1922.
Art Gallery of New South Wales, Sydney

Heysen's Birds (1923)
Wood engraving. 14.5 cm × 15.2 cm.
Art Gallery of South Australia, Adelaide

The Jester (1923)
(Self-portrait in Fancy Dress)
Wood engraving. 14.5 cm × 9.6 cm.
Ballarat Fine Art Gallery

Goat and Rhododendron (1925)
Wood engraving. 17.0 cm × 15.3 cm.
Mr Peter Lindsay, Sydney

Lethe Wharf (c. 1932)
Wood engraving. 32.5 cm × 17.3 cm.
Private Collection, Sydney

Roy Davies (born 1897)

L. Roy Davies began wood engraving in 1921. He exhibited twelve prints at Tyrrell's in Sydney in 1923 and works by him were illustrated in *Art in Australia* in the same year. He is described as 'one of the youngest artists to employ this medium [wood-engraving] . . . who has cut a considerable number of blocks'. Davies exhibited regularly in Sydney and was reproduced in *The New Woodcut*, a special issue of *Studio*, in 1930. Later, in 1948, he became principal of the National Art School in Sydney.

The Camp (1923)
Wood engraving. 5.4 cm × 9.8 cm.
Reproduced from *Art in Australia III*, no. 4, August 1923.

Napier Waller (1894–1971)

Mervyn Napier Waller studied at the National Gallery School in Melbourne under Bernard Hall. He married Christian Yandell in 1915 or 1916 and, shortly after, enlisted in the army and went to the front. His right arm was amputated after being wounded at Bullecourt, and while recuperating in England, he learnt to use his left arm for drawing. After his return to Australia he was the first artist to make linocuts in this country. A group of linocuts was exhibited in Melbourne in 1923, and two examples, the *Ring*, and *Guinea Fowls*, were included in the 1923 exhibition of Australian art in London. In the late 1920s he produced a small group of colour linocuts. Waller produced some fine watercolours and worked on mural paintings and mosaics, which establishes him as an outstanding neo-classical artist. From 1939 he also worked in stained glass. He and his wife Christian collaborated on some of his monumental projects.

Guinea Fowl (1923)
Linoleum cut. 11.0 cm × 14.5 cm.
Art Gallery of New South Wales, Sydney

Turkeys (1923)
Linoleum cut. 14.6 cm × 27.6 cm.
Art Gallery of New South Wales, Sydney

The Ring (1923)
(Sigurd)
Linoleum cut 27.6 cm × 21.1 cm.
Ballarat Fine Art Gallery

The Shepherd (1923)
Linoleum cut. 19.6 cm × 17.9 cm.
Art Gallery of New South Wales, Sydney

The Man in Black (c. 1928)
Colour linocut. 30.6 cm × 17.8 cm.
National Gallery of Victoria, Melbourne

The Labyrinth (1932)
Linocut. 24.4 cm × 20.4 cm.
National Gallery of Victoria, Melbourne

Christian Waller (c. 1895–c. 1952)

Christian Yandell was born to a Castlemaine pioneer family. She showed early promise and went to Melbourne in about 1912 to study at the National Gallery School. Several years later she was married to Napier Waller, a fellow student. Her book illustrations attracted favourable notice. She worked in increasingly close collaboration with her husband on his murals and mosaics, and after a visit to England in 1939 both turned their attention to designing and making stained glass. Christian Waller's outstanding graphic work is *The Great Breath*, an album published in Melbourne in 1932 and containing seven linocuts of symbolic designs presenting her religious philosophy. The two linocuts illustrated here are from this work.

The Golden Faun (1932)
Linocut. 31.8 cm × 13.7 cm.
From *The Great Breath*, 1932.
National Gallery of Victoria, Melbourne

The Lords of Venus (1932)
Linocut. 31.8 cm × 13.7 cm.
From *The Great Breath*, 1932.
National Gallery of Victoria, Melbourne

Frank Reynolds

Frank Reynolds worked in Melbourne and made a number of woodcuts of rustic and pastoral subjects in the 1920s. He may have worked as a newspaper illustrator. Biographical details are not at present available.

The Duck Pond
Woodcut. 19.9 cm × 19.4 cm.
National Gallery of Victoria, Melbourne

Hall Thorpe (1874–c. 1945)

In 1891 John Hall Thorpe was apprenticed in Sydney to John Fairfax and Sons. Here he learnt drawing and engraving on wood and became staff artist of the *Daily Mail*. He exhibited paintings with the Society of Artists. In 1902 he left for England, where he continued to work as an artist for several newspapers. By 1918 he had begun to make colour woodcuts and published pamphlets on their use for decoration. By the early 1920s he had established a successful studio for the production of his woodcuts, which achieved favourable critical notice and popular success not only in England but in a number of countries. Most of his woodcuts seems to date from the early 1920s. His colour woodcuts were advertised in Sydney in the late twenties and early thirties. He died in London towards the end of the Second World War.

Piccadilly (c. 1922)
Colour woodcut. 16.2 cm × 19.2 cm.
Rev. H. Peak, Sydney

Margaret Preston (1875–1963)

Margaret Rose MacPherson was born in Adelaide and she studied there and at the National Gallery School in Melbourne before travelling to Europe. She studied in Munich then went to Paris and London. During the war she taught at the Seale Hayne Military Hospital. In 1919 she returned to Australia and married W. G. Preston. She is said to have exhibited colour woodcuts in London in 1913. After her return to Australia she became active in this medium and had large exhibitions of woodcuts in 1925 and 1929. By 1930 she had made over one hundred woodcuts. As her subject matter she choose native flora and fauna particularly but also landscapes and street scenes in and around Sydney. An increasing awareness and appreciation of Aboriginal art shows itself in her prints as well as in her writings. As yet, research has not established her entire output of woodcuts, which must number several hundred.

Lorikeets (1925)
Woodcut, hand-coloured. 24.7 cm × 24.9 cm.
Australian National Gallery, Canberra

Macquarie St Sydney (c. 1925)
Woodcut. 12.0 cm × 12.5 cm.
Mr Christopher Davis, Sydney

Nude (1925)
Woodcut. 12.4 cm × 25.0 cm.
Australian National Gallery, Canberra

Black Swans, Wallis Lake (c. 1925)
Woodcut. 19.4 cm × 27.2 cm.
National Trust of Australia (N.S.W.)

Circular Quay (c. 1925)
Woodcut. 24.4 cm × 28.8 cm.
Mr Christopher Davis, Sydney

Mosman Bridge (large) N.S.W. (c. 1926)
Woodcut, hand-coloured. 25.2 cm × 18.7 cm.
Private collection, Sydney

Balmoral Beach N.S.W. (c. 1926)
Woodcut, hand-coloured. 30.2 cm × 22.4 cm.
Shepparton Art Gallery, Victoria

Shell Cove, Sydney (late 1920s)
Woodcut, hand-tinted. 21.7 cm × 27.2 cm.
Australian National Gallery, Canberra.

Wheel Flower (1928)
Woodcut, hand-coloured. 44.1 cm × 44.7 cm.
Art Gallery of New South Wales, Sydney

Original Wood Block for Wheel Flower (1928)
Art Gallery of New South Wales, Sydney

Waratahs (c. 1930)
Woodcut, hand-coloured. 30.0 cm × 42.5 cm.
Mr Christopher Davis, Sydney

Native Everlastings, N.S.W. (early 1930s)
Woodcut, hand-coloured. 43.4 cm × 38.0 cm.
Art Gallery of New South Wales, Sydney

Banksias
Woodcut. 30.5 cm × 30.4 cm.
Art Gallery of New South Wales, Sydney

Aboriginal Bark Ornament (1940 or 1946?)
Woodcut. 35.5 cm × 34.8 cm. Printed on tapa cloth.
Australian National Gallery, Canberra

Thea Proctor (1879–1966)

Thea Proctor studied in Sydney with Julian Ashton and exhibited paintings and posters with the Society of Artists before travelling to London in 1903. During her eighteen years in London she developed into a fine watercolourist and draughtsman and worked in lithography with the Senefelder Club, achieving considerable distinction in this medium. She returned to Australia in 1921. Her first woodcuts were made in 1925 on blocks of wood given to her by Margaret Preston. They were intended as decorations for children's nurseries.

In the later 1920s Thea Proctor had an important influence as a teacher of woodcut and linocut. Works by her students were reproduced in several issues of *Art in Australia* and some are shown in this book. She herself does not seem to have made any woodcuts after 1932.

The Swing (1925)
Woodcut, hand-coloured.
Art Gallery of New South Wales, Sydney

The Rose (c. 1928)
Woodcut, hand-coloured. 22.1 cm × 20.9 cm.
Ballarat Fine Art Gallery

Bonnets, Shawls, Gay Parasols (c. 1930)
Woodcut. 27.9 cm × 24.3 cm.
Private collection, Sydney

Summer (c. 1930)
Woodcut, hand-coloured. 17.4 cm × 22.8 cm.
Art Gallery of New South Wales, Sydney

The Sonnet (before 1932)
Woodcut, hand-coloured 12.5 cm × 12.4 cm
Australian National Gallery, Canberra

Ailsa Lee Brown (1899–c. 1945)

Ailsa Lee Brown, born Ailsa Craig, was a student of Thea Proctor in the late 1920s. She held a pilot's licence. After the death of her first husband she married the aviator 'Scotty' Allan and moved to Brisbane for two years (1935–1936). She and her husband then returned to Sydney and settled at Palm Beach. She worked on woodcuts through the thirties and early forties, her later work being signed Ailsa Allan. She died in an accident at Palm Beach towards the end of the war.

Moths Around the Quay (1932)
Linocut. 19.6 cm × 22.9 cm.
The National Trust of Australia (N.S.W.)

Gladys Gibbons (1903–1969)
Gladys Walker was born in Sydney on Christmas Day 1903. She studied at Julian Ashton's school and married the painter Henry Gibbons, who later became head of the school. While a pupil of Thea Proctor, she produced linocuts and woodcuts, a number of which were reproduced in *Art in Australia* from 1927 to 1929. She admired the work of Gwen Raverat, Eric Gill and other English woodcut artists. She also worked in watercolours.

In the Gardens (1928)
Linocut. 15.9 cm × 18.7 cm.
The National Trust of Australia (N.S.W.)

Still Life (early 1930s?)
Linocut. 16.4 cm × 16.0 cm.
Art Gallery of New South Wales, Sydney

Adrian Feint (1894–1971)

Adrian Feint first studied at Julian Ashton's school and was a student of Thea Proctor in the late 1920s, when some of linocuts and woodcuts were reproduced in *Art in Australia*. He enjoyed an active career as a painter, commercial artist and designer, and he made a number of etchings. He is particularly noted for his fine book plates and book illustrations and for his flower paintings.

Dinner Party—illustrations for a book (late 1930s)
Wood engraving. 7.7 cm × 10.2 cm.
Ballarat Fine Art Gallery

Amy Kingston (born 1912)

Amy Kingston studied in Hobart with Mildred Lovett, who inspired in her student an interest in simple shapes and forms. She then moved to Sydney where she became a student of Thea Proctor in 1933 and part of 1934. The small number of linocuts produced in the mid-thirties show Thea Proctor's influence on pattern and texture. From 1937 to 1940 she was in London studying at the Slade School, where she concentrated on stage design. She then returned to Australia where she achieved note as a stage designer.

Ship's Ventilators—Bass Strait Crossing (c. 1933)
Linocut. 16.7 cm × 13.6 cm.
Art Gallery of New South Wales, Sydney

Adelaide Perry (1900–1973)

Adelaide Perry studied at the National Gallery School in Melbourne and later in London and Paris. On her return she settled in Sydney, where she established her own art school. She was admired as a fine draughtsman as well as a painter, and a small number of her woodcuts and linocuts, some used for book illustrations, are known.

Kurrajong (c. 1929)
(The Citrus Orchard)
Woodcut. 15.1 cm × 22.3 cm.
Art Gallery of New South Wales, Sydney

Vera Blackburn (born c. 1911)

After studying at Sydney University, Vera Blackburn became a student of Adelaide Perry and produced a number of linocuts. In 1934 she left Sydney and travelled to England, where she studied at the Westminster Art School. She married and settled in England and did not pursue a career as an artist.

Lake of Swans (early 1930s)
Linocut. 30.2 cm × 24.5 cm.
National Trust of Australia (N.S.W.)

Pattern (1936)
Linocut. 27.6 cm × 26.9 cm.
Mrs P. M. Game, Kent, England

Raymond McGrath (born 1903)

Raymond McGrath was active in producing woodcuts in Sydney in the 1920s. He was also trained as an architect, and in 1928 left Australia to study at Clare College, Cambridge.

Babette S'en Va (1928)
Wood engraving. 10.3 cm × 12.7 cm.
Art Gallery of New South Wales, Sydney

Rah Fizelle (1891–1964)

Rah Fizelle is remembered as a distinguished painter, watercolourist and draughtsman and was the founder, with Grace Crowley, of an important school of avant-garde art. Only a handful of woodcuts by him are known. These were probably made in London in about 1930 under the influence of Frank Medworth, then a teacher at the Westminster School of Art.

Rooster and Hens (c. 1931)
Woodcut. 7.6 cm × 10.3 cm.
Newcastle City Art Gallery

Gladys Owen (1889–1960)

Gladys Owen was born in Sydney where she studied at Dattilo Rubbo's school. She later studied in London at the Grosvenor School of Modern Art. A number of woodcuts of European scenes were exhibited and reproduced in the early 1930s. She married the architect John D. Moore.

Gubbio in Umbria (c. 1930)
Woodcut. 11.1 cm × 15.8 cm.
Newcastle City Art Gallery

Maude Sherwood (1880–1956)

Born in New Zealand, Maude Sherwood studied there and in Paris and came to Australia in 1915. She later travelled extensively in Europe, returning to Australia in 1933. She was a painter and watercolourist as well as a printmaker.

Anemones
Colour linocut. 24.1 cm × 20.9 cm.
Art Gallery of New South Wales, Sydney

Dorrit Black (1891–1951)

Dorothea Black was born in South Australia and studied art in Adelaide under H. P. Gill. In 1915 she moved to Sydney to study at Julian Ashton's school. Her paintings were exhibited in Sydney from 1916. In 1927 she left for England, where she studied for three months at the Grosvenor Art School. Her use of linocut begins at this time and shows strong influence from her teacher, Claude Flight. Dorrit Black returned to Sydney in late 1929. She later returned to Adelaide, where she built herself a studio.

The Pot Plant (1933)
Colour linocut. 30.5 cm × 19 cm.
Art Gallery of South Australia, Adelaide.

Ethleen Palmer (c. 1908–c. 1965)

Ethleen Palmer exhibited with Macquarie Galleries in the late 1930s and was the subject of an article 'An Australian Hokusai?' in *Art in Australia*. She taught at East Sydney Technical College and was one of the first Sydney artists to work extensively in screen printing in the late 1940s. She later retired to live in the Blue Mountains. Her earlier works remain her most interesting.

Boat & Moon (late 1930s?)
Colour linocut. 15.2 cm × 15.3 cm.
Mr Rodney de Soos, Paddington

Pouter Pigeons (late 1930s)
Colour linocut.
Art Gallery of South Australia, Adelaide

E. L. Spowers (1890–1947)

Ethel Spowers first studied briefly in Paris with Delécluse in 1910. On her return to Melbourne she studied at the National Gallery Art School under Bernard Hall. From 1921 to 1924 she was in Paris and London. She studied at the Académie Rauson and the Regent Street Polytechnic and began working in colour woodcut. She returned to London in 1928 and studied at the Grosvenor School of Modern Art, which revolutionized her work. The example of Claude Flight and his followers almost certainly influenced her use of colour linocut, which was to become her special medium. Miss Spowers was a founding member of the *Melbourne Contemporary Artists* in 1932, as well as a member of the *Victorian Artists Society*. When her print *Wet Afternoon* was first exhibited it was described as her masterpiece. A companion print, *The Newsboy*, is less well known but equally striking. She worked also in oil and watercolour, and towards the end of her life she illustrated a number of books for children. Her best works are strikingly modern for their time, and in some cases were perhaps too modern for her audience, causing her to destroy many of her works. Until recent years her work had been sadly neglected.

Afraid of the Dark (1927)
Woodcut. 16.1 cm × 15.1 cm.
National Gallery of Victoria, Melbourne

Still Life (1929)
Wood engraving. 10.3 cm × 12.7 cm.
Art Gallery of New South Wales, Sydney

Wet Afternoon (1930)
Colour linocut. 24.1 cm × 20.2 cm.
Art Gallery of New South Wales, Sydney

Children's Hoops (c. 1932)
Colour linocut. 19.7 cm × 26.1 cm.
National Gallery of Victoria, Melbourne

E. W. Syme (c. 1890–1961)

Eveline Syme was a contemporary and friend of Ethel Spowers. Few biographical details are available, but it is probable that she studied in England. She was a founding member of *Melbourne Contemporary Artists* in 1932 and exhibited until 1936. She travelled extensively, and her subject matter includes Hong Kong harbour.

The Castle Chapel, Amboise (late 1920s?)
Linocut. 10.2 cm × 14.1 cm.
Art Gallery of New South Wales, Sydney

Mabel Pye (born 1894)

Mabel Pye was a fellow student of Napier Waller and Adelaide Perry at the National Gallery Art School, Melbourne, where her work attracted attention. She became a member of the Victorian Artists Society and regularly exhibited paintings and watercolours with fellow members. She was also a member of the Society of Woman Artists. Her linocuts were made mostly in the late 1930s. She continued to exhibit until 1957.

Woman by a Window (late 1930s?)
Colour linocut. 14.6 cm × 17.1 cm. Printed on blotting paper.
Dr Robin Sharwood, Melbourne

Will Dyson (1880–1938)

Will Dyson is best remembered for his political cartoons, which were published in a number of newspapers. He made a series of lithographs of World War One subjects and in the 1930s he made a number of very witty drypoints on topical subjects, among them Sigmund Freud's psychoanalysis and Henry James. The woodcut shown here is an unusual example of his work, and was perhaps influenced by his brother-in-law, Lionel Lindsay, who had married Will's sister, Jean Dyson.

Spanish Dancer (before 1938, perhaps late 1920s)
Woodcut 22.4 cm × 13.7 cm.
National Gallery of Victoria, Melbourne

Murray Griffin (born 1903)

Murray Griffin, a Melbourne painter, was for many years an art teacher. By 1935 he was admired for his colour linocuts of birds, which were printed in strong colours with dense oily inks. Examples were reproduced in *Art in Australia* of that year. He has continued working in this medium. His best known works depict birds.

The Enchanted Wood (c. 1930)
Linocut. 17.0 cm × 22.1 cm.
National Gallery of Victoria, Melbourne

Ludwig Hirschfeld Mack (1893–1965)

Hirschfeld Mack was not, strictly speaking, an Australian artist. He was born in Frankfurt and he became a student in the printing workshop at the Weimar Bauhaus. He later became one of the Bauhaus teachers. At the outbreak of war he was in London; in 1940 he was deported to Australia where he was interned as a German alien at Hay and then at Tatura. During his internment he produced a small number of woodcuts, and after his appointment as art master at Geelong Grammar these, and some more recent woodcuts of scenes around Corio, were printed on the school's press and sold to assist the Russian Allied Armies in the war. While outside the general development of woodcuts in Australia, these prints show the direct influence of German expressionism.

Landscape, Hay (1940–1941)
Woodcut 13.0 cm × 18.0 cm.
Art Gallery of New South Wales, Sydney. (Gift of Mrs L. Hirschfeld, 1974)

James Flett (born 1906)

James Flett studied at night classes at the National Gallery School in Melbourne and began exhibiting colour linocuts in 1928. He cut a number of illustrations for books. His striking watercolours also attracted attention. He ceased making linocuts in the mid-thirties. He was a war artist during the Second World War, after which he turned to commerce.

The Artist (1928)
Colour linocut. 27.1 cm × 19.2 cm.
National Gallery of Victoria, Melbourne

Helen Ogilvie (born 1902)

Helen Ogilvie studied at the National Gallery School in Melbourne under Bernard Hall. After leaving the school and finding employment she began, after 1930, to make linocuts in her free time and to exhibit them. Later, she took up wood engraving when she discovered a book on wood engraving by Eric Gill's teacher, Beedham, and some steel engraving tools in a cutler's shop. Her first work in this medium was exhibited in 1935. After the Second World War she turned her attention to painting and has become known for her delicate studies of old outback buildings.

Chooks in the Straw (c. 1932)
Colour linocut. 15.1 cm × 20.9 cm.
National Gallery of Victoria, Melbourne

Eric Thake (born 1904)

Eric Thake was apprenticed to the artists' department in a process engraving firm in Melbourne. He attended night classes at the Gallery Art School, and in 1935 he began engraving on stereotyping metal. His succinct and elegant book plates won him recognition. He turned increasingly to linocut, a medium that he has continued to use. He first exhibited in 1929 with Eveline Syme, Ethel Spowers and Dorrit Black. He still makes a linocut each year as his personal Christmas card. Thake uses oil, watercolour and the camera with great distinction and very individual style. His work is characterized by fine and incisive draughtsmanship coupled with an unusual and sharp perception and wry humour.

Family Group (1930)
Linocut, hand-coloured. 17.5 cm × 13.0 cm.
Made for Dr and Mrs Clive Stephen.
Private collection, Sydney

Cold Iron (1932)
Linocut. 25.3 cm × 20.0 cm.
Newcastle City Art Gallery

The Bird of Heaven (1932)
Linocut. 25.7 cm × 21.3 cm.
Illustration for *Moby Dick*.
National Gallery of Victoria, Melbourne

Crucifixion (1936)
Linocut. 27.7 cm × 19.1 cm.
Art Gallery of New South Wales, Sydney

Strange Spectacle (1944)
Linocut (Christmas card): sheet. 13.3 cm × 16.0 cm.
Australian National Gallery, Canberra

A Print from Johnny Fawkner's Press (1902)
Woodcut by Blamire Young

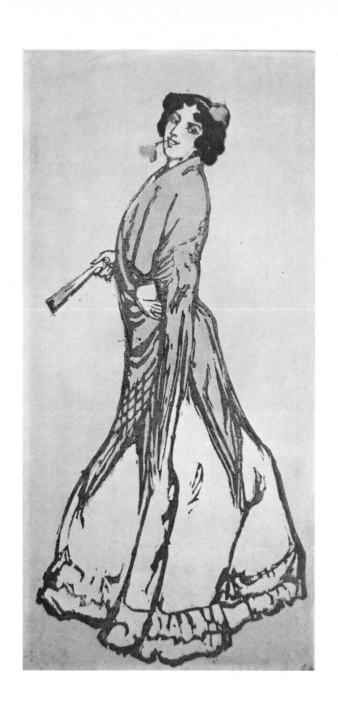

Spanish Woman (c. 1907)
Colour woodcut by Lionel Lindsay

Heysen's Birds (1923)
Wood engraving by Lionel Lindsay

Goat and Rhododendron (1925)
Wood engraving by Lionel Lindsay

Lethe Wharf (c. 1932)
Wood engraving by Lionel Lindsay

The Camp (1923)
Wood engraving by Roy Davies

Guinea Fowl (1923)
Linoleum cut by Napier Waller

Turkeys (1923)
Linoleum cut by Napier Waller

The Ring (1923)
(Sigurd)
Linoleum cut by Napier Waller

The Shepherd (1923)
Linoleum cut by Napier Waller

The Labyrinth (1932)
Linocut by Napier Waller

The Golden Faun (1932)
Linocut by Christian Waller

The Lords of Venus (1932)
Linocut by Christian Waller

The Duck Pond
Woodcut by G. F. Reynolds

Lorikeets (1925)
Hand-coloured woodcut by Margaret Preston

Macquarie St Sydney (c. 1925)
Woodcut by Margaret Preston

Nude (1925)
Woodcut by Margaret Preston

The Man in Black (c. 1928)
Colour linocut by Napier Waller

Piccadilly (c. 1922)
Colour woodcut by Hall Thorpe

Mosman Bridge (large) N.S.W. (c. 1926)
Hand-coloured woodcut by Margaret Preston

Wheel Flower (1928)
Hand-coloured woodcut by Margaret Preston

Original wood block for Wheel Flower (1928)
By Margaret Preston

Native Everlastings, N.S.W. (early 1930s)
Hand-coloured woodcut by Margaret Preston

The Swing (1925)
Hand-coloured woodcut by Thea Proctor

The Rose (c. 1928)
Hand-coloured woodcut by Thea Proctor

Summer (c. 1930)
Hand-coloured woodcut by Thea Proctor

Anemones
Colour linocut by Maude Sherwood

The Pot Plant (1933)
Colour linocut by Dorrit Black

Boat & Moon (late 1930s?)
Colour linocut by Ethleen Palmer

Wet Afternoon (1930)
Colour linocut by E. L. Spowers

Woman by a Window (late 1930s?)
Colour linocut by Mabel Pye

The Artist (1928)
Colour linocut by James Flett

Chooks in the Straw (c. 1932)
Colour linocut by Helen Ogilvie

Family Group (1930)
Hand-coloured linocut by Eric Thake

48

Black Swans, Wallis Lake (c. 1925)
Woodcut by Margaret Preston

Circular Quay (c. 1925)
Woodcut by Margaret Preston

50

Balmoral Beach N.S.W. (c. 1926)
Hand-coloured woodcut by Margaret Preston

Shell Cove, Sydney (late 1920s)
Hand-tinted woodcut by Margaret Preston

Banksias
Woodcut by Margaret Preston

Aboriginal Bark Ornament (1940 or 1946?)
Woodcut on tapa cloth by Margaret Preston

Bonnets, Shawls, Gay Parasols (c. 1930)
Woodcut by Thea Proctor

The Sonnet (before 1932)
Hand-coloured woodcut by Thea Proctor

Moths Around the Quay (1932)
Linocut by Ailsa Lee Brown

In the Gardens (1928)
Linocut by Gladys Gibbons

Still Life (early 1930s?)
Linocut by Gladys Gibbons

Dinner Party (late 1930s)
Wood engraving by Adrian Feint

Ship's Ventilators—Bass Strait Crossing (c. 1933)
Linocut by Amy Kingston

Kurrajong (c. 1929)
(The Citrus Orchard)
Woodcut by Adelaide Perry

Lake of Swans (early 1930s)
Linocut by Vera Blackburn

Pattern (1936)
Linocut by Vera Blackburn

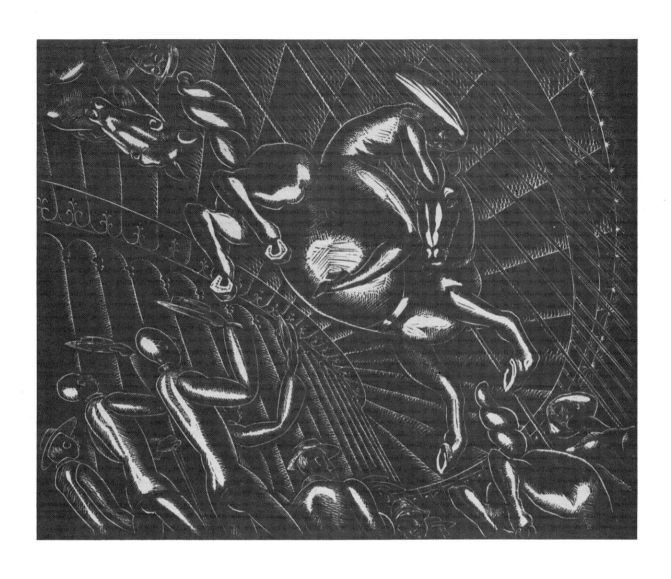

Babette S'en Va (1928)
Wood engraving by Raymond McGrath

Rooster and Hens (c. 1931)
Woodcut by Rah Fizelle

Gubbio in Umbria (c. 1930)
Woodcut by Gladys Owen

Pouter Pigeons (late 1930s)
Colour linocut by Ethleen Palmer

Afraid of the Dark (1927)
Woodcut by E. L. Spowers

Still Life (1929)
Wood engraving by Ethel Spowers

Children's Hoops (c. 1932)
Colour linocut by E. L. Spowers

The Castle Chapel, Amboise (late 1920s?)
Linocut by E. W. Syme

Spanish Dancer (before 1938 perhaps late 1920s)
Woodcut by Will Dyson

The Enchanted Wood (c. 1930)
Linocut by Murray Griffin

Landscape, Hay (1940–1941)
Woodcut by L. Hirschfeld Mack

Cold Iron (1932)
Linocut by Eric Thake

The Bird of Heaven (1932)
Linocut by Eric Thake
Illustration for *Moby Dick*.

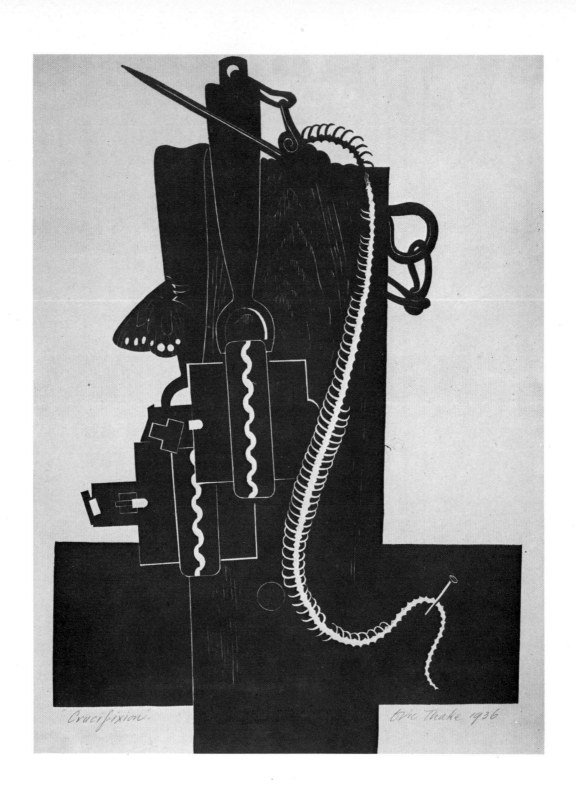

Crucifixion (1936)
Linocut by Eric Thake

Strange Spectacle (1944)
Linocut by Eric Thake

Acknowledgments

I am deeply indebted to the artists whose works appear in this book and, in particular, to Mr Eric Thake and Miss Helen Ogilvie; and to the relatives and friends of other artists, not only for permission to reproduce works but for ready help, advice and encouragement. Mrs Clive Bennett, formerly Treania Smith, gave generous help with collection of material and assessment of works.

My many friends and colleagues in public galleries have given freely their time, advice and help. In particular, I would like to thank Misses Sonia Dean and Irena Zdanowicz of the National Gallery of Victoria, Messrs Barry Pearce and Ian North of the Art Gallery of South Australia, Mr Andy Fergusson of Newcastle City Art Gallery, Mr Jim Mollison and Mrs MacKean Taylor of the Australian National Gallery, Mr Ron Radford of the Ballarat Fine Art Gallery, Mr Peter Timms of the Shepparton Art Gallery, and Miss Margaret Rich of the Geelong Art Gallery. I am also very grateful to their various institutions for readily making available photographs of works in their collections. The National Trust of Australia (N.S.W.) has also supplied prints from their collection. Mr David Liddle has patiently and ably photographed additional material.

Mr Christopher Davis and other private collectors kindly gave me ready access to works in their possession. Mr Frank MacDonald, whose interest in the subject and period rivals my own, has provided valuable stimulus and help. My colleagues Mr Daniel Thomas and Miss Frances McCarthy read my text and provided useful suggestions. Mr Cedric Flower has acted as a benevolent Svengali during the preparation of this book. Miss Kerry Reardon willingly deciphered my illegible scrawl and typed the manuscript.

To all who have contributed to this book I express my gratitude.